ALL ABOUT PROFESSIONAL FOOTBALL

FANTASY FOOTBALL

FANTASY FOOTBALL CHEAT

Player	NFL Team	B W
	GB	10
Aaron Rodgers	NO	10
Drew Brees	IND	7
Peyton	NE	
	DAL	

MC

by James Buckley, Jr.

FANTASY FOOTBALL

by James Buckley, Jr.

Mason Crest
450 Parkway Drive, Suite D
Broomall, PA 19008
www.masoncrest.com

Printed and bound in the United States of America.

Series ISBN: 978-1-4222-3576-8
Hardback ISBN: 978-1-4222-3577-5
EBook ISBN: 978-1-4222-8300-4

First printing
1 3 5 7 9 8 6 4 2

Produced by Shoreline Publishing Group LLC
Santa Barbara, California
Editorial Director: James Buckley Jr.
Designer: Bill Madrid
Production: Sandy Gordon
www.shorelinepublishing.com
Cover photographs: Tom Croke/Icon SMI/Newscom (Gronk); Cliff Welch/Icon Sporting News/ Newscom (Martin); Scott Anderson/Dreamstime (Rodgers); Joshua Daniels/Dreamstime (paper).

Library of Congress Cataloging-in-Publication Data is on file with the Publisher.

CONTENTS

Key Icons to Look For

Words to Understand: These words with their easy-to-understand definitions will increase the reader's understanding of the text, while building vocabulary skills.

Sidebars: This boxed material within the main text allows readers to build knowledge, gain insights, explore possibilities, and broaden their perspectives by weaving together additional information to provide realistic and holistic perspectives.

Educational Videos: Readers can view videos by scanning our QR codes, providing them with additional educational content to supplement the text. Examples include news coverage, moments in history, speeches, iconic sports moments and much more!

Text-Dependent Questions: These questions send the reader back to the text for more careful attention to the evidence presented here.

Research Projects: Readers are pointed toward areas of further inquiry connected to each chapter. Suggestions are provided for projects that encourage deeper research and analysis.

Series Glossary of Key Terms: This back-of-the-book glossary contains terminology used throughout this series. Words found here increase the reader's ability to read and comprehend higher-level books and articles in this field.

INTRODUCTION

Are these Baltimore Ravens fans happy because their team's kicker made a field goal? Or because he's on their fantasy football team?

ANOTHER WAY OF CHEERING

A Green Bay Packers fan goes nuts when Jay Cutler, the quarterback for the Packers' archrival Chicago Bears throws a touchdown pass. A Houston Texans fan dances around his living room when a Dallas Cowboys running back runs for a score. A Seattle Seahawks fan hangs his head when a Seattle kicker makes a long field goal.

What's going on here?

Those fans are watching sports in a very different way than most fans. They are cheering not for the teams on the field, but the teams in their head and on their computers and mobile devices. They are cheering for fantasy teams.

Fantasy football has completely changed the way that NFL fans watch games these days. In fantasy football, a person chooses a lineup of real-life NFL players. He (or she) then matches that lineup against another fan-chosen team within his (or her) fantasy league. The stats put up on TV by the NFL stars turn into points for the fantasy teams, and like in an NFL stadium, one team comes out the winner. By focusing on the stats of individual players instead of the Ws put up by entire NFL teams, fans now watch every game with a new focus: How is this helping me?

Some say that fantasy sports—now a billion-dollar industry all by itself that includes just about every pro sport you can think of—has played a huge role in making the NFL by far the largest sports league in the country and one of the biggest in the world. TV rights fees have skyrocketed in the past decade. Is that because more fans want to watch more games, even those that don't involve their hometown heroes? Fantasy football is why a Week 15 matchup between two 3-12 teams might bring in huge ratings, just because a star running back is piling up points for fantasy teams around the country.

History

Fantasy sports have been a big part of American sports in general since fantasy baseball began in the early 1980s. A group of New York sportswriters gathered at a French restaurant called La Rotisserie Francaise and created their own baseball league, with teams made up of players in the Major Leagues. Their teams then performed based on the stats built up by the "real-life" Ma-

jor Leaguers. A year later, they wrote about a book about what they called "Rotisserie Baseball," after the restaurant name. It became fantasy baseball and set off a sports revolution. Fantasy football was soon part of the mix, and other sports were added as the years went on. As we'll see, by the 2000s, fantasy sports had created enormous changes in how sports are covered, watched, and reported, to say nothing of how they are enjoyed by tens of millions of fans.

However, fantasy football has a secret—and, actually, older—history. In 1962, a group of writers and officials working around the Oakland Raiders, then part of the American Football League, got together in a New York hotel room. After an evening of planning and plotting led by a Raiders part-owner named Bill Winkenbach, they came up with the Greater Oakland Professional Pigskin Prognosticators League (GOPPPL). Pigskin is a nickname for a football, while prognosticators is a fancy word for "predictors." After the first draft in 1963, GOPPPL had eight teams. The participants kept the league pretty much to themselves in the early years, but by the 1970s it had expanded, thanks to one of the team owners also owning a bar.

After the fantasy baseball craze started, fantasy football became popular, too, even though the guys in Oakland were already veterans. By 1989, more than 1 million people were playing the game. With the beginning of the Internet in the 1990s, those numbers went through the roof.

"I'm continually astounded by what has happened to it," said original GOPPPL member Scotty Stirling on NFL.com.

He's not the only one. By 2015, more than 56 million people were playing some form of fantasy sports, with football being the dominant sport. Fantasy sports were creating fun, competition, and increased interest in the game and its players. In 2015, however, another form of the game also caused enormous controversy. Newer "daily" games were turning fantasy into an unpleasant reality. However, time will tell whether that is a blip in the rise of fantasy or the crack in the mirror that takes away the fun. In the meantime, read on to find out how to play, and how something that's not "real" has become the biggest thing in football.

Wayback Machine! Fantasy football history.

"I can't even imagine watching the NFL without having some fantasy interest now," says Michael Fabiano, senior fantasy analyst on NFL.com. "People feel like they're more a part of the game, more a part of the NFL, because they manage those players they see on TV. Before fantasy football, you were rooting for the team you've always followed. Now, you're following every team."

CHAPTER 1

Real football coaches can call the plays and have an influence on the game. Fantasy coaches pick and watch.

FANTASY FOOTBALL BASICS

Chances are, you are not a football coach. You probably are not the general manager of a team, either. You probably will never have the chance to tell a $15 million quarterback that he's on the bench this weekend or that a Pro Bowl wide receiver just doesn't have good numbers against a particular defense. Well, that might be true in real life, but in fantasy football, all those dreams can come true.

Fantasy football teams give everyday fans the chance to create their own teams. They don't have to sit back and just watch the annual NFL Draft…they have their own draft. They don't have to yell at the TV after their favorite team's player fumbles, they can bench

Words To Understand

special teams divisions of a football team that take part in all plays that are not part of a defensive or offensive formation, such as kickoffs and punts

waivers a process in the NFL that allows teams to let players go and pick up players who are not on another team

that guy next Sunday! The dream of actually playing in the NFL comes true for only a tiny fraction of people who love the game. However, the dream of owning and running a team, if only on paper

Preparing for a fantasy football draft calls for research, research, research.

(or should we say "on screen"?) now comes true every week of the NFL season for millions of people.

This chapter assumes that you know what NFL football is, but that you're just learning about fantasy football. If you're a fantasy football expert, feel free to skim (but remember, this information might be on the test!).

Fantasy Basics

In fantasy football, a team owner is in a small league of fellow fantasy owners. Each owner chooses a set of NFL players to be on his or her team. That fantasy team then racks up points based on how the real

NFL players do. If Doug Martin of the Buccaneers scores a touchdown and he's on Buckley's Bashers, then Buckley gets six points…as do the Bucs. The flip side, of course, is that if star receiver Julio Jones of the Falcons has a bad day and he's also on the Bashers, then Buckley is not a Jones fan that day. Like the Falcons' real-life coach, he has to just watch and wail.

NFL and fantasy players earn points for scoring touchdowns, making field goals, and racking up yardage. Defensive points come from limiting opponents to points, making interceptions, or, of course, scoring touchdowns. Quarterbacks get points for touchdown passes, passing yards, and rushing touchdowns. They also lose points for throwing interceptions. The value of those points changes depending on the type of league you choose; there are many variations (see further on).

Each week, two fantasy teams play each other. Whichever team gets the most points is the winner. At the end of the regular season in most leagues, the teams with

Getting Started: Tips on beginning to play fantasy

the best records face off in playoffs to determine a league champion. After the final game, as in the NFL, the winner is celebrated as the best of the best and can lord it over his friends…until next season starts.

Getting Started

The first step in fantasy football is to form the league. You need to gather at least seven other friends (or groups of friends; many teams have co-owners) to join you. Most fantasy leagues have 10 or 12 teams. It should be an even number because each week, teams from your league match up in pairs, just like they do in the NFL. (So, yes, there is a reason there are 32 NFL teams and not 33.)

Once you have agreed on who is in the league, you'll choose one of the many websites that will "host" your league. CBS Sports, Yahoo!, ESPN, NFL.com, and many others are out there. Shop around and see which one you like the best. Some are completely free, while others charge fees that offer added treats. Most now have mobile apps as well so that you can keep track of your team whenever you're connected.

It's important to note here the difference between "weekly" and "daily" fantasy football. Much more will be written later about the daily version. What we're describing here is the weekly version, the much older and

more popular style of the game. The fantasy teams put together in this weekly version are basically the same from week to week throughout the season. The money paid is simply a fee to the host site, and the winner does not get any money back. (Private betting among friends can be a part of this, but minors should not do any gambling for money.) In daily fantasy, as we'll see, the line between having fun and gambling is blurry, and becoming blurrier each year.

Thank goodness for the Internet, say fantasy owners. Websites make keeping track of stats a snap.

The Draft

The league begins with a draft of players. The order of who picks first is usually assigned randomly. Team owners then take turns choosing players for their team. Most drafts run like a snake. That is, the team that drafts last then makes another selection and the order runs backward to the team that drafted first, and so on. This helps balance out the advantage gained by teams that had the very earliest picks.

Though the rules vary by league, most call for certain positions to be filled. Each fantasy team typically has a quarterback, two running backs, two wide receivers, a tight end, a kicker, and a defensive/**special teams** entry. (That last entry is an entire NFL team that piles up points for the owner when that team is on defense and when it earns points on special teams, such as with kickoff return touchdowns.) Most leagues also add a "flex" position that can be an additional receiver, running back, or tight end. Most leagues also then have reserves on the "bench."

Kickers are not the biggest guys on the field, but they contribute many points to fantasy teams.

During the season, owners can move players from the bench to the starting lineup. Only players in the starting lineup earn points during a weekend's games.

The draft is often where leagues have the most fun. Some gather the owners in a room. Fortified with pizza and snacks, owners choose their teams, taking time with each pick to let the owner know just what they thought about it! Draft Day can often turn into a great event for friends and family, perhaps ending with watching an actual NFL game!

Other drafts are held online, with players in various locations making their picks on the league's website. In both cases, the team owners have been—for hours, days, or even weeks—researching the players they will pick. As we'll see in Chapter 3, an entire industry has grown around fantasy sports, with plenty of experts ready to tell you how to draft.

Other Leagues

Most players are in a basic, weekly, 10- to 12-team league. There are some other options.

• Keepers: Owners can keep a few of their players from year to year, thus building their teams as NFL franchises do.

• PPR Leagues: This type has most of the usual scoring but gives players extra power by giving them points for every reception they make. Thus a running back who also catches passes is a valuable two-way threat.

• IDP Leagues: In this league, owners chose individual defensive players instead of a whole team. They earn points for tackles, turnovers, sacks, etc.

Playing the Game

Once your team is set up, you choose the players for your starting lineup for the first week's game. You might look at what NFL teams your players are facing, or what the weather will be. If your kicker does better indoors than outdoors, should you make sure he only plays for you in domed stadiums? Does your running back's opponent have a great run defense? Should you play an extra wide receiver this week, or make your "flex" spot a tight end? You also need to watch for player injuries and player news. Is an NFL coach making a change to his starting lineup that will affect yours? Is a player's injury not healing in time?

Just like a real team's coach and general manager, the decisions are up to you. Choosing a lineup each week is one of the most important, and most fun, parts of being a fantasy team owner. Most leagues let you make changes right up until kickoff of a player's "real" game, so apps and mobile devices have become a key part of every fantasy owner's tool kit.

Once the real games begin, you sit back and watch. Or, if you're like many owners, you sit on the edge of your seat with your phone handy awaiting texts with news of your players' achievements. You'll watch the points build up as the games progress. With the final whistle of the Monday-night game, the fantasy weekend is over. If your team racked up more points than your opponent, you won. If not, better luck next week.

Trading and the Waiver Wire

In between the weekend's games, the fantasy owner's work doesn't stop. Like an NFL team, a fantasy team can change its lineup and its roster as the season moves on. Not every NFL player will be on a fantasy team in your league, so there are always options to swap in rising stars or to replace injured players. To do this, you hunt the waiver wire. **Waivers** is a process in the NFL that allows teams to let players

NFL.com named Cleveland tight end Gary Barnidge the top waiver-wire pickup of the 2015 season, thanks to his unexpected success.

go and pick up players who are not on another team. In fantasy, it works mostly the same way. Each week the pool of available players ("free agents") is open to all teams in your league. Those who want a particular player make a "claim" online. Usually, the site will award the players to teams with the lowest ranking to that point in the season. That way, teams that are not doing well have a chance to get better players, while teams that are already succeeding have to wait a bit.

A team with struggling wide receivers might try to trade for a solid scorer like Arizona's Anquan Boldin.

Another way to change your team, hopefully for the better, is by trading. You can offer a trade to any other owner in your league, again via the website. You can also call or email, of course, and negotiate before you make an official offer. If a trade is accepted, your players leave, and the new players arrive. Then you fit them into your lineup however you want. For many owners, the ongoing, in-season movement of players is a large part of the fun of fantasy.

Winning

Now for the really fun part: winning. Each week, you'll put together the team you think gives you the best chance to win. If your guys come through for you, that's just what happens. As the season goes

If your team had Jacksonville's Blake Bortles in Week 16 of the 2015 season, you were very happy with his 29 fantasy points.

on and the wins pile up, you can start getting ready for the playoffs. Fantasy playoffs usually take part in the latter weeks of the NFL regular season. Regular fantasy can't continue in the NFL playoffs because not all teams and their players are available for fantasy play. So weeks 15, 16, and sometimes 17 are the tense ones for fantasy owners. They might look weeks ahead to see how NFL teams are matching up and make trades or waiver pickups with an eye on those games.

Finally, after a season of trades, free agents, wins, and maybe losses, you end the final Monday with the most points in the championship game. Then you really know what the Super Bowl champ feels like ... but without all the confetti or the trip to Disney World. This is still fantasy football, after all!

 # Text-Dependent Questions

1. Name three ways that NFL players score points for a fantasy team.

2. How do you get a player on waivers?

3. What is a "sleeper"?

 # Research Project

Check out the major websites that run fantasy leagues. Which appeal to you the most? Do you like how Site A sets up its draft? Or do you prefer Site B's free research? Pick a site that you think would be best for your fantasy league.

CHAPTER 2

Early fantasy players loved high-scoring players like the Cowboys' Emmitt Smith, who led the NFL in touchdowns three times.

GROWTH OF THE GAME

Fantasy football took a while to make its big impact on the NFL at large. Those early pioneers with GOPPPL were barely known outside the San Francisco Bay Area. Even when the concept of fantasy sports became more mainstream in the late 1980s, fantasy football was seen as being for nerdy outsiders. You had to be a complete football fanatic to want to go through the effort needed to deal with all those stats.

Just finding the stats to research players was a burden. Even in the 1980s, the level of information about players, stats, trends, and more was low for fans, and limited mostly to NFL insiders in

Words To Understand

crawl in broadcasting, the term for the words and information that move across the bottom of a screen while another program plays above

mainstream the general and more popular direction in which a culture is going

revenue total money taken in by businesses

team front offices. Fantasy fans had magazines and newsletters they could read, and annuals came out with rankings of players. But there was no one-stop shopping spot. That changed in the 1990s.

Internet Changes the Game

As it did with just about everything else in the world, the Internet changed fantasy football completely. Until websites were available to anyone with a connection to the Internet, fans had to keep all their stats by hand. They used calculators and spreadsheets and notebooks and wall charts. Suddenly, it seemed, they could sit at their computer and have a machine do all the work—except picking the players, of course.

The first World Wide Web browsers came along in the middle of the 1990s. The NFL started its own website, NFL.com, in 1995. And in 1997, CBS Sports presented the first website dedicated to fantasy football leagues. With shocking speed, the web spread fantasy football to millions of new players. No longer were league organizers responsible for keeping stats and deciding about waiver claims. Now it was all done with the click of a mouse.

"The Internet made things so much easier for fans to take part," says NFL.com senior fantasy analyst Michael Fabiano. "It's so simple now. All the scoring and stats are done for you."

The NFL was initially worried about doing its own version of fantasy (see sidebar). But it watched as other services and companies charged ahead and got strong footholds in the market. Once the NFL got over its early reluctance, it jumped in with both feet. However, it waited too long, and a golden opportunity was lost. In the early "Wild West" days of the Internet, there was little policing of the information. The first companies to set up fantasy sports sites just grabbed all the information they could, used it, and gathered customers.

An Inside Story

This author was part of the editorial team that helped start NFL.com, and was already playing both fantasy baseball and football. He suggested strongly that the league include fantasy on the new site in some way. His idea was shot down as presenting the chance of being "perceived as gambling." Of course that was something no pro sport league could touch with a 10-foot pole. Even though he explained the difference between fantasy and gambling, the NFL said no… then. By the 2000s, it had seen the light and created an enormous fantasy section on the site, and published an annual magazine, whose editor was…this author.

The Courts Help the Fans

In 2006, Major League Baseball went to court to prevent fantasy leagues from using MLB's statistical information and player names. They felt that those groups were making money on an MLB product without paying for that right. Needless to say, the NFL and other pro sports leagues watched this case with great interest. The NFL was in the fantasy game through its own website, making money on the ads sold on pages that fans viewed. But if they could force other sites to pay them a fee for that information, it would increase **revenue** dramatically.

MLB, however, lost that case. A judge ruled that they could not prevent fantasy sites from using stats and player names, though the sites could not use official league logos or marks. But fantasy players didn't need the logos; they just needed the info and were thrilled by the win.

The NFL joined MLB in recognizing that particular cat was out of the bag. In the following years, the NFL jumped even further into the fantasy pool. Since the league could not charge for the information, it began to charge for expertise. Through Time Inc. Magazines, the NFL published an annual magazine, the *NFL.com Fantasy Football Preview*. (This author was an editor of that publication for six years.) It began a series of online NFL Fantasy shows. It hired experts and began making them household names.

As the popular weekly fantasy games grew—and before the specter of daily fantasy got in the way—the league clearly recognized why the whole idea worked.

"Even if your team isn't playing well," NFL commissioner Roger Goodell said, "you're still following your fantasy league or you're following the [NFL TV show called] Red Zone or your mobile device."

The NFL has taken the position that weekly fantasy greatly adds to a fans' enjoyment, and it's constantly working on ways to take advantage of that.

The NFL's official fantasy guide was one of many publications aimed at the growing legion of owners.

Congress Keeps the Door Open

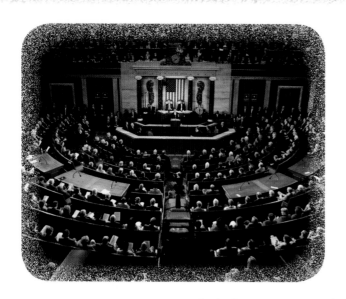

Action by Congress in 2006 has played a huge role in expanding fantasy, while opening up the "daily" loophole.

The same year as the stats court case from MLB, Congress got involved and opened the door wider for non-league-approved fantasy sports. The Unlawful Internet Gambling Enforcement Act was passed to prevent online poker and other clear gambling sites from setting up on the web. Fantasy sports were not mentioned at all. They were considered to be a game that called for skill—owners had to do research to choose the right players to win—and not chance, such as card games.

That's the key difference between gambling and fantasy sports of all kinds. The other is whether money is at risk with each play in the game. As we'll see in Chapter 4, however, that difference can be blurry when you play "daily" fantasy sports.

Gambling depends on luck; you don't get to have any personal impact on whether or not the Rams beat the Chiefs. However, in fantasy, you are making the decisions of what players to choose, what players to start that weekend, and what trades or player move to make. That makes it a game of "skill," according to most people. That is, you have to do work and research and make decisions that affect the outcome, even though that outcome still has a big element of chance—that is, what happens on the real-life grass and turf fields of the NFL.

With the loophole that allowed fantasy sports online to stay legal, participation skyrocketed. In 2006, about 10 million people played. By 2015, it was nearing 60 million people, spending almost $3 billion on the game in fees and, as we'll see, possibly on gambling.

Media Coverage Changes

With the rise of fantasy, the way that the NFL is covered by the media has also changed greatly. No longer are sports highlight shows simply showing video of the best plays of the day. Now nearly every show has a constant **crawl** of information showing

How fantasy has affected media coverage of pro fooball

how individual players did that day, a sure sign that fantasy players are watching. By the mid-2000s, reporters were asking players if fans should draft them for fantasy teams, and making jokes about how a bad day "hurt all those fantasy teams." Some players ran with the joke, others resented it, but everyone was and is talking about it throughout the NFL season.

Those media outlets also became sources of advice from newly minted fantasy experts hired by the networks. Often they were former math wizards or statistically minded people who were better with a calculator than a football playbook. They analyzed players not necessarily for their strength or football moves, but for the sheer numbers they put, the patterns they made, and the fantasy results they produced. No longer is it enough to say who won the game; the media now has to make sure fantasy owners know how their players did, too.

Huge numbers of fantasy players now also use mobile apps that send texts or messages every time one of their team puts up a point, or if that week's opponent pulls ahead. Sunday (and Monday night and the occasional Thursday or Saturday) now means a constant watch on the very small screen, awaiting every nugget of news about a team that only exists on that screen.

Fantasy sports has attracted fans young and old of all genders, expanding the NFL's fan base.

And the game is pulling in new fans, too. At a 2015 fantasy sports event (yes, they have those), Michael Beller of *Sports Illustrated* was quoted as saying, "That is really where [fantasy] has really changed—just how many people are playing. Even ten years ago it was diehard sports fans [who played], and now the one friend you grew up with who wasn't into sports is playing fantasy football."

Players Play, Too

How'd you like to own a fantasy team and draft yourself to play on it? That's the case for many NFL players who own fantasy teams. Then again, you might have a shot at putting someone better than you in the same spot. Then what do you do: cut yourself from the team?

Almost from the beginning, NFL players have enjoyed playing fantasy football. Some have really gotten into it, writing online columns with advice or describing how they picked their teams with fellow NFLers. Players in other sports are into it as well; many Major League Baseball teams have fantasy leagues among their players.

In 2015, Cleveland Browns tight end Ben Tate had extra fun with fantasy, as he played in a league organized with Browns fans. He picked his team and played them all one at a time. He showed that he knows as much about fantasy as he does about reality by looking at Mr. Everything Cam Newton as a possible No. 1 overall pick.

It's not just players, either. NFL.com's Fabiano notes that famed CBS Sports broadcaster Jim Nantz has become a big fantasy fan. Fabiano reports that

Nantz tells him that the research he does for his team helps him with his work on-air.

When you've got real-life players picking themselves and real-life announcers learning stats by drafting teams, you know that fantasy football is a permanent part of the NFL fabric.

 # Text-Dependent Questions

1. Why was the NFL reluctant, at first, to get involved with fantasy football?

2. What league lost a key court case that opened up fantasy sports even more?

3. Describe in a few words how fantasy has changed NFL media coverage.

 # Research Project

Do some research on the growth of fantasy sports participation. (The Find Out More section has some good starting points.) Make a chart or a graph showing the rise in total numbers over the past 15 years.

CHAPTER 3

At the NFL Honors show, Pittsburgh's Antonio Brown took home
the award as top fantasy performer for the 2015 season.

The Business of Fantasy

The games may be fantasy, but the money is very, very real. The Fantasy Sports Trade Association (FSTA) estimates that annual spending on fantasy sports in general tops $2.6 billion per year. That includes fees that fans spend to run their leagues, money they spend to get good advice, time spent traveling for the drafts, and other expenses.

For most fans, the payback for that expense is simply fun and competition. Daily fantasy players are making up a larger and larger share of that pie; we'll talk more about that a bit later. But if most of the fantasy players are not making the money on fantasy football, who is?

Words To Understand

lucrative something that produces a great amount of money

obsessed thinking or talking about someone or something to an extreme

Show Them the Money

The first place to look is at the websites that host the leagues. Some offer a basic league for free, and make money on the ads that appear on the many, many pages that owners spend time looking at as the season progresses. Others have those ads, but also charge a fee to a league—usually divided up among all the owners—for providing statistical and hosting services. Since the vast majority of those are automated, for the websites it's a high-profit deal.

Fantasy football has meant big money for networks, websites, and the NFL.

George Leimer runs fantasy sports for ESPN. He says that the NFL fantasy season brings 17 percent of the site's daily traffic. That's about 90 million visitors a month. For that reason, ESPN has built up a robust fantasy advice operation, offering many articles before and during each sport's season. By paying the extra "Insider" monthly fee, fans can get even more such advice from experts such as Matthew Berry (see below).

CBS Sports is another major player in fantasy sports, offering baseball, football, basketball, and hockey versions. They offer different levels of service, some for a fee, some for free, and all creating page views of ads that generate income for the site.

Expert Advice–for a Fee

The next area of expense for a fantasy owner—and of revenue for the "experts"— is fans that pay for advice and inside information about NFL players and teams. An entire line of business has grown up in recent years among journalists, writers, and analysts. They make their living advising fantasy team owners about which players to draft, which trades to make, and which trends to follow. These experts are usually paid by the websites out of fees

Not Just for Guys

According to an American Express survey in 2015, more than one in five fantasy football players were women. That's more than 15 million females taking part in an activity tied to a sport that is traditionally male-dominated. The ability of fantasy players of any gender to study numbers and stats makes the game accessible. You don't have to be an expert on zone defenses or pro-set offenses to enjoy and succeed in fantasy football. And the fun and ease of cheering for "your" guys appeals to people of all ages. Perhaps more than any other NFL program, fantasy sports has broadened the league's appeal.

Show them the money:
Inside the business of fantasy

and advertising revenue. Some have set themselves up to be paid directly. Fans are willing to shell out cash to help their teams. For weekly players, that probably won't result in any sort of payoff. For the growing number of daily players, it's another investment in their ongoing attempts to hit the jackpot.

Michael Fabiano is an example of one of those experts. Since 2006, he has worked for NFL.com as its Senior Fantasy Analyst. He wrote for the league's preview magazine, but that soon became a sidelight, as his presence on NFL.com grew from just writing to appearing on regular video segments. The birth of the cable-TV NFL Network greatly expanded his work and his audience.

He has seen the game grow enormously, perhaps most clearly in attracting what the NFL calls the "casual" fan.

"My sister is a perfect example," says Fabiano. "She didn't like football as we were growing up. First, I 'poisoned' her over to the Dallas Cowboys. And now she's **obsessed** with fantasy football. She plays in five leagues. In my position, I've seen lots of celebrities play—we have an NFL league of TV and movie stars. I run a team for New York Yankees' catcher Brian Mc-Cann. It's become something that everyone just does every season."

Over on ESPN, Matthew Berry is one of that network's "big-name" experts. A former TV comedy writer, he has built a fol-lowing with columns and TV appearances that are entertaining as well as informative. He started writing for Rotoworld.com as a sideline, but soon it became a full-time job. In 2007, he joined ESPN, where he is known as The Talented Mr. Roto, and advises fans on football and baseball. He also has a popular podcast.

Berry and Fabiano are just two of many such "experts" who have found steady and **lucrative** work telling fantasy owners who the latest sleepers are or what running back has the potential to become this week's breakout star. CBS, Yahoo, and other sites all

NFL.com's Michael Fabiano is one of many experts who have made fantasy advice a career.

Too Young to Play

The NFL started a mini-version of fantasy football on its NFL Rush site aimed at kids 14 and under. Though the kids might have had fun, some people felt that it was too much, too soon. In 2016, anti-gambling groups wrote to the NFL asking that they stop offering fantasy to youngsters. Keith Whyte, executive director of the Washington, D.C.-based National Council on Problem Gambling, wrote that such games "may encourage children to spend excessive amounts of time trying to win prizes, planting the seeds of addiction." The NFL said that parents had to approve kids taking part in the online contest.

have their experts, too. Turns out that obsessing about sports stats as a kid can actually pay off with a job…for a lucky few.

Daily Fantasy Shows Up

Websites, ads, expert fees, and more (there are even fantasy sports conventions and special trips to games!): It all adds up to several billion dollars a year. While all that money sounds like a lot, the creation of another kind of fantasy football in 2009 changed the game . . . again. By 2013, more than a million people were playing a form of the game that called for daily (or in the NFL's case, weekly) drafts. Players paid a fee for each game they got in. Unlike the weekly game, in this case, players could win money—more than $1 million in some rare cases—

if they successfully picked a winning fantasy team. While at first glance that sounds like a big bonus for fantasy players, instead it has opened up an enormous controversy about the role of gambling in sports.

 ## Text-Dependent Questions

1. What is the name of the group that provides information about fantasy sports to the media?

2. What was Matthew Berry's job before he became a fantasy sports writer?

3. Why are some people opposed to youngsters playing fantasy football?

 ## Research Project

Read columns by several online fantasy football experts. Do you think they present their information well? See if you can find them talking about similar players and compare (or contrast) what they say about that player. Do you have a favorite expert after your research?

CHAPTER 4

DRAFT KINGS

MOBILE FOOD VENDOR
CITYWIDE
NOT TRANSFERABLE
NYC

C 3655
THREE SIX FIVE FIVE

APPLY INSERT HERE
EXPIRES IN MONTH / YEAR PUNCHED:
☐ 2014 ☐ 2015
APPLY INSERT HERE

JAN. FEB. MAR. APR. MAY. JUN.
JUL. AUG. SEPT. OCT. NOV. DEC.

COMPLAINTS? Call 311

Play for free and win millions. What could go wrong? Fans found that it was not quite that easy; governments agreed.

PLAY FREE

1-WEEK FANTASY FOOTBALL

THE DAILY FANTASY CONTROVERSY

If you followed the NFL in 2015, you could not escape the ads. Two companies, FanDuel and DraftKings, seemed to be having a commercial war on every NFL broadcast and on every TV sports show. Add in millions of ads on websites, and it was a bigger blitz than any linebacker ever made. What was going on?

"Daily" fantasy was making its pitch for fans' dollars…in a big way. In the space of one NFL season, daily fantasy created an

Words To Understand

fleece to take money from by deception

implied suggested indirectly

insider trading the use of information known only to members of a company to make a financial profit

investors people who commit money to a project in the hopes of receiving a greater financial reward from that project in the future

enormous controversy. On one side were fans who wanted to jump on the bandwagon that was turning everyday players into millionaires (though very rarely). On the other were anti-gambling forces that believed the sites were taking advantage of people. The major difference between the "traditional" fantasy football and daily—or in football's case, weekly—was that players changed their teams every weekend. The other major difference is that in daily fantasy, large chunks of money were ending up in winning team owners' hands. Suddenly, fantasy sports could pay off with real cash.

What Is Daily Fantasy?

In traditional fantasy football, an owner plays for a whole season before he or she knows if she's a winner. They match up the same basic team week to week, making changes here and there, but not starting from scratch every weekend. In "daily" fantasy, the owner starts from scratch every weekend, building a new team that racks up points. (In other sports, the name makes more sense, since baseball and basketball, for example, play nearly every day of the week in their respective sports.)

Unlike in weekly fantasy football, owners in daily fantasy can share players because the choice is not by drafting, but by meeting a salary cap. That is, after paying an entry fee (more on that in a moment), players then build their team by combining the pre-determined salaries of players until they have reached the game's pre-assigned salary cap. For example, one game might allow a $50,000 total to be spent on a team to fill eight positions. The fantasy owner has to mix and match players, looking for bargains or taking risks on high-salary stars, until the positions are filled and no more salary cap room is left. Then the owner watches that team play against what could be thousands of others in the same game. Only one of those thousands can win each week and take home the big prizes. Teams finishing

The dueling daily fantasy sites spent millions putting their logos on everything they could, including sports courts.

near the top can also get a small payday. For the rest of the folks, it's "goodbye money."

"It's a new season every week," according to FanDuel owners.

However, as we'll see, those simple rules open up a complicated question. Is daily fantasy a game of skill? You need to do research, study facts, and form your own team based on knowledge. Or is it a form of gambling, based mostly on luck? That is, while you might be able to choose which NFL players are on your team, you have no way of changing the outcomes of their actual games; that is, you don't call the plays, make the throws, or block the kicks. In traditional fantasy, the money you pay goes as a fee that you know you won't get back. You are paying for the service of hosting the team, running the website, or providing expert advice. If you win, you get to rule over your friends, but you don't take home money from the website. In daily fantasy, that game changes. If you win, you actually take more money than you put into that particular game. The website, however, still keeps a percentage of the money that is bet, so it wins no matter what. Everyone else in that game that you won loses the money they wagered.

The Big Splash

At the beginning of the 2014 NFL season, about $1 million was available to players on the two major daily fantasy sites: FanDuel and DraftKings. As the season went on, however, that pot grew steadily. The operators saw that this was possibly going to become even bigger when some of their end-of-season events drew a lot of media attention. For FanDuel's final championship, with the winner to get $2 million, the organizers held it live in Las Vegas and broadcast it online. Scenes of the dancing, celebrating champ clearly had a big affect on future players. Those scenes were repeated in a series of ads that began in the summer. The ads told the story of how a pair of brothers from Boston put in $35 and a week later won $2 million, thanks to their choice of an obscure running back named Jonah Gray who came out of nowhere to score four touchdowns in one game.

The possibility that daily fantasy would grow attracted **investors**. NFL owners such as Jerry Jones of Dallas and Robert Kraft of New England put in their own money for part-ownership. The National Hockey League and the National Basketball Association quickly jumped in with sponsorship deals. Major League Baseball took part-ownership in DraftKings.

The operators of those two sites made their own big bet heading into the 2015 season. In August, they spent tens of millions of dollars on advertising that blanketed the sports world. According to *Sports Illustrated*, in September, the two companies spent more on ads than all the beer companies combined. In the sports world, that's really saying something. A commercial featuring the brothers appeared 32,000 times before the 2015 season. DraftKings answered back by running more than 46,000 ads.

ESPN The Magazine reported that an ad for daily fantasy was on about every 90 seconds for more than a month. DraftKings even had a marketing deal with sports powerhouse ESPN, so their logo—and ESPN's **implied** support—was all over the network, its sites, and its app.

Jerry Jones of the Cowboys was one of several sports figures to invest in the future of daily fantasy sports.

After a summer and fall packed with ads for the games, the prize pool had risen to a stunning total of more than $800 million between the two sites. Not surprisingly, that brought in even more players. They were attracted by ads showing "regular" guys becoming millionaires after paying $5 to set up a team.

Those Boston brothers did indeed win their money. But that was one story out of millions. It is like playing the lottery. Yes, someone wins. Maybe a couple of someones. But in the end, all but a tiny handful of players lose the money they put into the game, whether that's "daily" NFL fantasy or the state lottery. Like a running back being tripped up by a fast-moving defender, daily fantasy was heading for the end zone when it was tackled.

Daily Takes a Big Hit

Perhaps the biggest blow that daily fantasy sites took in that fast-moving 2015 season was their own fault. In early October, news began to filter out that an employee of DraftKings was doing more than making websites and writing text. He used data available only to employees to create teams that brought him more than $350,000 in winnings…on FanDuel, the rival site. This kind of **"insider trading"** immediately gave the daily sites a big black eye. If the everyday players were competing against insider experts with information not available to the public, how was that fair?

Both sites quickly passed rules that banned employees from playing on either site, but the damage was done. The blitz of ads and the relatively few "big" winners began to be seen for what it was: a marketing deal to bring in people's money with little chance of their getting it out. Daily fantasy was quickly perceived not so much as a fun thing based on good research, but a real form of gambling. And in nearly every place in the United States, gambling is illegal. The question remained, however: Is daily fantasy football (or any daily fantasy sports) illegal gambling?

The Government Strikes Back

The controversy of insider playing, along with the stunning and rapid rise of daily fantasy, quickly caught the attention of various parts of the government. The two sites were working in a gray area of the law, and state governments acted quickly to make things black-and-white again. Five states already had laws on their books calling daily fantasy sports play "gambling," and banned the practice. Those included Arizona, Iowa, Louisiana, Montana, and Washington.

The competition's rapid rise in the 2015 season raised eyebrows. In October 2015, the U.S. Congress called for an investigation by the Federal Trade Commission, with an eye toward making sure consumers were not being ripped off.

New York state attorney general Eric Schneiderman was one of the leaders of the movement to ban daily games.

During the presidential campaign, candidates were asked about it during nationally televised debates.

That month, one state fired another damaging shot against daily fantasy. Nevada is home to Las Vegas and Reno, two cities where gambling of all sorts is not only legal, but celebrated. However, Nevada felt that daily fantasy was the same thing and thus banned it, unless it would agree to be regulated by the state as the other gambling games are.

A month later, the New York state attorney general told both sites that they could no longer accept money from New York state residents. The sites closed down access for New York after state attorney general Eric Schneiderman wrote this: "DraftKings and FanDuel are the leaders of a massive, multibillion-dollar scheme intended to evade the law and **fleece** sports fans across the country."

In December, Illinois became the latest state to make daily fantasy sports illegal. Attorney general Lisa Madigan said that people playing daily fantasy are no different than bettors in Nevada laying out money on which team will win a game by how many points.

Not every state opposes fantasy sports. In January 2016, the California Assembly easily passed a bill that would license fantasy sports in the state. Leaders of the state's many pro teams all supported the bill. "Fantasy sports has been an important tool used to deepen connections and engagement with our fans," wrote Los Angeles Clippers vice president Pete Thuresson to the Assembly.

At press time, the bill was proceeding to the State Senate. However, since only one Assemblyman voted against it, passage seemed likely.

California and other states that are considering joining, rather than fighting, daily fantasy sports are hoping that by having some control, they can keep the abuses down. Groups opposed to gambling and organizations that help people with gambling problems naturally feel that the bill is a bad idea.

For its part, the NFL is remaining neutral. Says NFL.com's Michael Fabiano: "The NFL hasn't yet embraced that fully. But that was the case with traditional fantasy, too, so who knows what will happen in the future? In any case, daily fantasy has grown the popularity of fantasy sports in general. It appeals to some people who get frustrated with the long-term nature of the traditional fantasy format."

NFL Players React

NFL players have long had a love-hate relationship with fantasy football. When it first started, it was sort of cute. As it grew larger and larger, they wondered if they were missing out on a payday. Some sites and games created official licensing deals with the players to send them a cut of profits. The 2006 court case, however, meant that most fantasy games didn't need to get players' or teams' permissions to use the publicly available stats.

The daily game, however, was perceived as different. It is not a game played for private winnings or for a plastic trophy. A handful of players were making huge sums, while the two main sites were raking in enormous profits. In October 2015, Washington Redskins wide receiver Pierre Garçon led a lawsuit against the two sites. The claim was that FanDuel and Draft-Kings were using the players' names without permission and without paying for that right. That court case continued into 2016, but clearly showed that the daily fantasy sites had another big problem on their hands.

Meanwhile, DraftKings solved that problem. In 2015, they signed a deal with the NFL Players Association, the union representing all NFL players. The

Washington's Pierre Garcon was the leader in a suit by NFL players to stop daily sites.

deal basically paid cash to every player for the use of their names in the games.

What's Next?

The future for daily fantasy football is murky. It continues to be played regularly in baseball and basketball, where there are many more games each day than football's weekly slate of 12 to 16 contests. However, the numbers of people playing those other sports is well below that of football. So as each NFL season dawns, and as more and more states make new rules, just how popular will daily fantasy continue to be? Will more fans realize what *The New York Times* journalist Gregg Easterbrook, a longtime NFL observer, wrote in 2014: "DraftKings and FanDuel seduce men and women into a dream of instant wealth. A handful do achieve instant wealth; for most, this dream only worsens inequality."

For most fans, and certainly fans younger than 21, daily fantasy sites should be approached with extreme caution if at all. Traditional weekly fantasy football games can be a great way to add enjoyment and fun to a fan's love of pro football; daily games can become more than that…in the wrong direction.

Of course, you can always just skip the fantasy and enjoy the reality. Put on your favorite team T-shirt and just cheer for a real-life team to win.

 # Text-Dependent Questions

1. What is a typical salary cap in daily fantasy football?

2. Name an NFL owner who invested in a daily site.

3. Why are states banning daily fantasy football?

 # Research Project

Read articles about both sides of the daily issue. Do you think it's truly gambling? Or is it still a game of skill that calls for research and planning more than just luck?

FIND OUT MORE

Books

Chandler, Brett. *How to Beat Your Friends at Fantasy Football: A Complete Beginner's Guide.* Amazon Digital Services, 2015.

Ordine, Bill. *Fantasy Sports: Real Money.* Las Vegas: Huntington Publishing, 2015.

Websites

fsta.org
The Fantasy Sports Trade Association has pages of material that talk about how great fantasy sports are. Of course, they are not unbiased!

nfl.com/fantasy
The NFL runs its official fantasy site packed with leagues to join, videos to watch, and commentary from experts. CBS Sports and ESPN are other places to go to join basically free fantasy football leagues.

sportingnews.com/fantasy
One of America's oldest sports publications has long been a source of up-to-date fantasy information for its readers.

bleacherreport.com
This online-only site has a bit of an edge to it, mixing lots of opinions with some traditional sports reporting.

Publishers Note: The Publisher does not condone or encourage sports gambling. Gambling can strain relationships, interfere with work, and lead to financial catastrophe. Please consult applicable state and federal gambling laws.

SERIES GLOSSARY OF KEY TERMS

alma mater the school that someone attended

analytics in sports, using and evaluating data beyond traditional game statistics to predict a player's future success

brass a slang term for the high-ranking executives of an organization

bundling in television, the concept of customers paying for a set of cable channels with one set fee

bye weeks the weeks that NFL teams do not play a game; each team gets one bye week per season

credentialed provided with an official pass allowing entry into a private or restricted area

eligibility in this case, the right to continue to play on a college team, granted by both the school and the NCAA

endorsement support and praise offered by a paid spokesperson for a product or service

expansion team a new franchise that starts from scratch

feedback information used to improve something

general managers members of a sports team's front office in charge of building that club's roster

leverage the ability to direct the course of action in a decision

merger to combine into one

perennial occurring or returning every year; annually

protocol in this instance, a pre-planned series of steps or tests undertaken by medical professionals working with players

public relations the process of telling the public about a product, service, or event from the "company" point of view

red zone for the team with possession of the football, the area of the field from the opponents' 20-yard line to the goal line

special teams the kicking game in football: kickoffs, punts, field goals, and extra points

traumatic in medicine, describing an injury that is very significant, resulting in damage to body tissues

INDEX

CREDITS

(Dreamstime.com: DT; Newscom: NC) Lawrence Weselowski/DT 6; Andy Chu/TNS/NC 9; Hkratky/DT 12; Stevecuk/DollarPhoto 14; Joshua Daniels/DT 17; Lawrence Weselowski/DT 18; Robin Alam/Icon Sportswire/NC 21; Joe Robbins 22, 26; Tyler Kaufman/Icon Sportswire/NC 24; Katie Buckley/SPG 31; Wikimedia 32; Lisa F. Young/DT 35; John Salangsang/Invision for NFL/AP Images 38; NFL Photos 43; Justin Lane/EPA/NC 46; John Angelillo/UPI/NC 49; Gilbert Kueten/DT 50; Matthew Visinsky/Icon Sportswire/NC 53; Seth Venig/AP Photo 56; Daniel Kucin/Icon Sportswire/NC 59.

ABOUT THE AUTHOR

James Buckley Jr. is a former senior editor at NFL Publishing and was also the editor of the *NFL.com Fantasy Football Preview* magazine. He is the author of several books on pro football, as well as titles on many other sports. He has played fantasy football since the early 1990s… and, yes, he did win his league once.